Written and Illustrated
by Erinn Sneed

When I Grow Up Publishing, Inc.
Copyright © 2017 by Erinn Sneed
Written, illustrated and cover designed by Erinn Sneed
Edited by Anita Rose Banks and Sally Bennett

All rights reserved.
No part of this book may be photocopied, reproduced electronically or otherwise reproduced without prior written permission of the author.

Cleveland, Ohio


ISBN 978-0-9795117-4-5
0-9795117-4-7


Extra thanks to Elisha Patterson
who put me on the right path to veganism.

Thanks to Birdie from Shaker High School and
Adella from Kirk Junior High School
whose conversations influenced me to the path of vegetarianism.

Thanks to Anita Rose Banks and Sally Bennett.

# Contents

**Part 1** What's a Vegan? ...................................................................... 7

**Part 2** Vegan Recipes .......................................................................... 29
        Guacamole ............................................................................. 30
        Black Bean Chili .................................................................... 31
        Fruity Smoothie ..................................................................... 32
        Sweet Green Smoothie ........................................................ 32
        Chocolate Shake .................................................................. 32
        Scrambled Tofu .................................................................... 33
        Vegan Pizza .......................................................................... 33
        Chocolate Pudding .............................................................. 34
        Raw Oat Chocolate Chip Cookies ..................................... 34
        Vegan Cookbooks for Children .......................................... 35

**Part 3** Vegan Activities ...................................................................... 37
        Vegan Words ........................................................................ 38
        Fruits and Vegetables Puzzle ............................................. 39
        Famous Vegans Word Search ............................................ 40
        Maze ...................................................................................... 41
        Labyrinth ............................................................................... 42
        Answers ................................................................................. 43

**Part 4** Vegan Resource Guide .......................................................... 45
        Vegan alternatives to animal products............................. 46
        More vegan food alternatives to try ................................. 48
        Ingredients to watch for ..................................................... 49
        Vegan Cosmetics, Hygiene and Fashion ......................... 50
        The 8 Essential Amino Acids ............................................. 51
        Internet Resources for Vegan Information ...................... 51
        Food and Vegan Documentaries ...................................... 51
        Glossary ................................................................................ 52

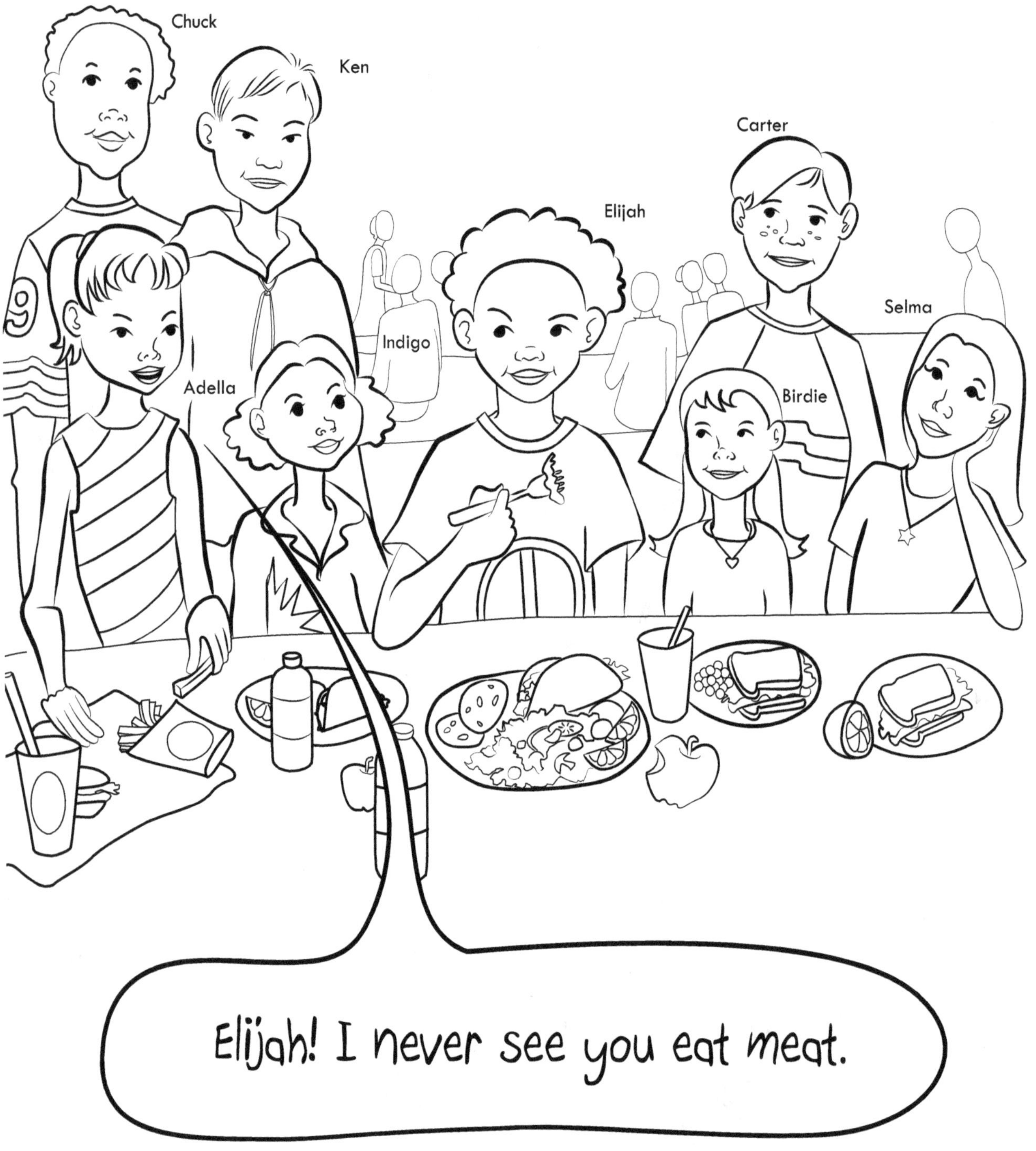

You see, plant foods contain amino acids, and that is what protein is made from. When you eat fruits, vegetables, nuts, seeds and grains, it's easy to get all the protein you need.

# Guacamole

**Serves about 4**
2 ripe avocados
1/4 onion
1/8 cup of fresh cilantro
juice of 1 lime or lemon
Dash of cumin
Dash of cayenne pepper
sea salt to taste

**Directions**
Cut the avocados in half, scoop out the flesh, and mash with potato masher or fork until creamy. Cut up onion and cilantro into small pieces. Add onions, cilantro, lime or lemon juice, cumin, cayenne and sea salt to avocado and stir. Dip with tortilla chips.

# Black Bean Chili

**Serves about 4**
1 can black beans
1 can tomato paste
1 cup textured vegetable protein (TVP)
1 cup water
1/2 onion
1/2 green pepper
1/2 cup mushrooms (optional)
1 sliced fresh tomato (optional)
2 T. chili powder
1/2 tsp. garlic powder
1/4 tsp. cumin
a dash or two cayenne pepper
1 T. olive oil
sea salt to taste

**Directions**
Heat black beans with water in a pot. When warm, add tomato paste and TVP. Allow to heat for 10 minutes. Add chopped onions, green peppers, mushrooms and tomatoes. Stir in chili powder, garlic powder, cumin, cayenne, olive oil and sea salt. Simmer for 5 minutes.

# Fruity Smoothie

**Serves 2**

2 bananas, frozen
1/2 cup strawberries, frozen
1/4 cup blueberries, frozen
3 or 4 dates, pitted
1/4 cup orange juice or apple juice

Place all ingredients in a high speed blender.

# Chocolate Shake

**Serves 2**

2 bananas
2 heaping T. carob powder
       or cacao powder
       or cocoa powder
1 cup almond milk
2 T. agave (or to taste)

Place all ingredients in blender. Blend on high speed.

# Sweet Green Smoothie

**Serves 2**

1/2 cup distilled water or fruit juice
2 bananas
2 apples
1 pear
1 kale leaf
3 or 4 dates, pitted
1 T. agave

Cut apple and pear into four sections and cut out the core. Place all ingredients in a high speed blender.

# Scrambled Tofu

**Serves 2**
1 firm tofu block
1/4 cup water
1/4 onion (medium size)
1/4 green pepper (medium size)
(or any color pepper you desire)
2 mushrooms sliced
1/2 celery stalk sliced
1 T. of olive oil (optional)
1/4 c. Daiya shredded cheese
(mozzarella flavor or your favorite flavor)
1 tsp. turmeric
sea salt to taste
dash of cayenne (optional)

Crumble up tofu and place in skillet with water. Cut up onion, pepper, mushrooms and celery. Place these veggies in the tofu. Then add olive oil and Daiya cheese into the skillet and mix. Add turmeric, sea salt and cayenne and stir. Allow to cook for 2-4 minutes.

# Vegan Pizza

**Serves 1**
pita bread
2-3 T. tomato sauce
1/4 c. Daiya shredded cheese
(mozzarella flavor)
1 T. olive oil (optional)
-------
All toppings are optional:
    chopped onions
    chopped olives
    chopped mushrooms
    chopped green peppers
    vegan pepperoni
    or your favorite vegan toppings

Place 2 tablespoons olive oil into a skillet on low heat. Place pita bread into skillet and warm both sides (1 minute each side). In another skillet, place one tablespoon of oil and add all sliced veggies. Heat for two minutes.

Cover pita bread with tomato sauce. Place the Daiya shredded mozzarella cheese on top of tomato sauce. Place veggies on top. Cook on low until cheese melts.

# Chocolate Pudding

**Serves 3**

3 large avocados, soft and ripe
1/4 cup cacao powder
    or cocoa powder
3-6 tablespoons coconut milk
1 tsp. vanilla extract
2 tsp. coconut oil
2 T. agave

Combine avocado, cacao powder, coconut milk, vanilla, coconut oil and agave in blender. Blend on high for 1 minute or until smooth.

Refrigerate for 30 minutes than serve.

# Raw Oat Chocolate Chip Cookies

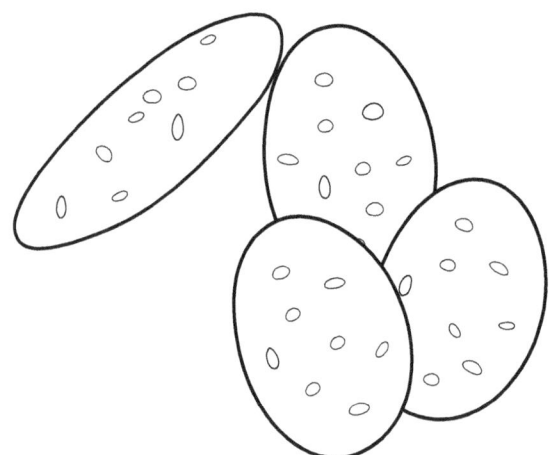

**Makes 4 large cookies**
1 cup oats
1 ripe banana
3/4 cup grated dry coconut
4 tsp. agave syrup
1 date, pitted
2 T. coconut oil
1/4 cup vegan chocolate chips

In a food processor, add the oats and pulse for 20 seconds in order to break the oats down. Add the rest of the ingredients (banana, coconut, date, agave and coconut oil) and pulse until fully combined. Mix in the chocolate chips. Refrigerate for 15 minutes or until stiff, then shape into small cookies and refrigerate until hard.

# Vegan Cookbooks for Children

Vegan Lunch Box by Jennifer McCann
Plant-Powered Families by Dreena Burton
The Plantiful Table by Andrea Duclos
The Help Yourself Cookbook for Kids by Ruby Roth
But My Family Would Never Eat Vegan! by Kristy Turner
How to Eat a Rainbow Vegan Recipes by Ellie Bedford
Kid-Friendly Vegan Cookbook by Richard West
Vegan Toddler Cookbook by Tory Archer
Vegan Cookbook for Kids by L.F. Boaventura

# Vegan Words

1. C _mp _ _ siona _e
2. S _stain _ _ili _y
3. Ani _al_
4. _e _eta _ _ es
5. N _t _
6. S _ _ d _
7. F _ _ i _
8. Ear _h
9. L _ve
10. G_ _i_s
11. _min_ A_i_s
12. Ca_ _ng

1. Compassionate, 2. Sustainability, 3. Animals, 4. Vegetables, 5. Nuts, 6. Seeds, 7. Fruit, 8. Earth, 9. Love, 10. Grains, 11. Amino Acids, 12. Caring

# Fruits and Vegetables puzzle

```
S B R O C C O L I C
P A S C H A R D A U
I S A M U L P R P C
N E N B N S R W P U
A G A W E O W E L M
C N N P T E L L E B
H A A S Y W T E S E
W R B K I W I S M R
G O T O M A T O E S
K A L E C U T T E L
```

apples
oranges
kiwi
grapes
lettuce
tomatoes

chard
kale
cucumbers
carrots
beets
broccoli

spinach
bananas
melon
plum

Answers on page 43

# Famous Vegans
## Word Search

This list is compiled from www.happycow.net

**Erykah Badu,** R&B singer

**Andre '3000' Benjamin,** musician from OutKast

**Linda Blair,** actress

**Tim Commerford,** musician in Rage Against the Machine

**Leonardo Da Vinci,** Italian painter and inventor

**Tony Gonzales,** NFL Star

**Joan Jett,** punk rock musician and singer

**Dennis Kucinich,** politician

**Carl Lewis,** ten-time Olympic medalist in Track & Field

**Ian MacKaye,** musician

**Jenny McCarthy,** actress, model

**Carrie Anne Moss,** actress in "The Matrix"

**River Phoenix,** actor

**Joanne Rose,** actor

**Geoff Rowley,** professional skateboarder

**Russell Simmons,** record company executive

**Stic.man,** musician in Dead Prez

**Ed Templeton,** professional skateboarder

**Vanessa A. Williams,** actress, dancer

```
E W E R D F N Y N Q T E K U V P B T Q V
A R S W E O R E W F R W I W U W I W A I
N C Y H T R A C C M Y N N E J M A N G H
I A W K W Q F R X L Y W J D C W E H Y A
J R W K A J A I C W R F A O J S L S N M
K R Y O A H W O S Q R W M B S R Y D Z U
L I E L K F B W C H M M W A U I R E U P
M E L M U O B A E W E U A S C E W N R O
N A W B C L K M D R W W S N B F W N W S
O N O G I J A W F U I E I E T Y E I F H
P N R M L N T O G L L V N G R T D S X R
S E F T B Q R W L L A J D W I I T K I O
E M F G V D R I S D A W N M A L E U N E
L O O H H W A I O M T Q H K L U M C E T
A S E K W M M D I E W G Q O B R P I O S
Z S G S S M R N Y W S G Y U A F L N H M
N W G M O A W A F G D I K T D G E I P I
O F K N N R K S S G B W W A N I T C R S
G C S O W C E Z R V R Y W E I P O H E T
Y W E W A D W N V N U T N T L C N W V T
N L W M S C A W N G N G K U P L W W I E
O W N L K T H M N A M C I T S A R W R B
T A S X C U P W P O O O W O C P Z A W L
I J O A N J E T T A W J B Y U L Y A C E
```

Answers on page 43

# Maze

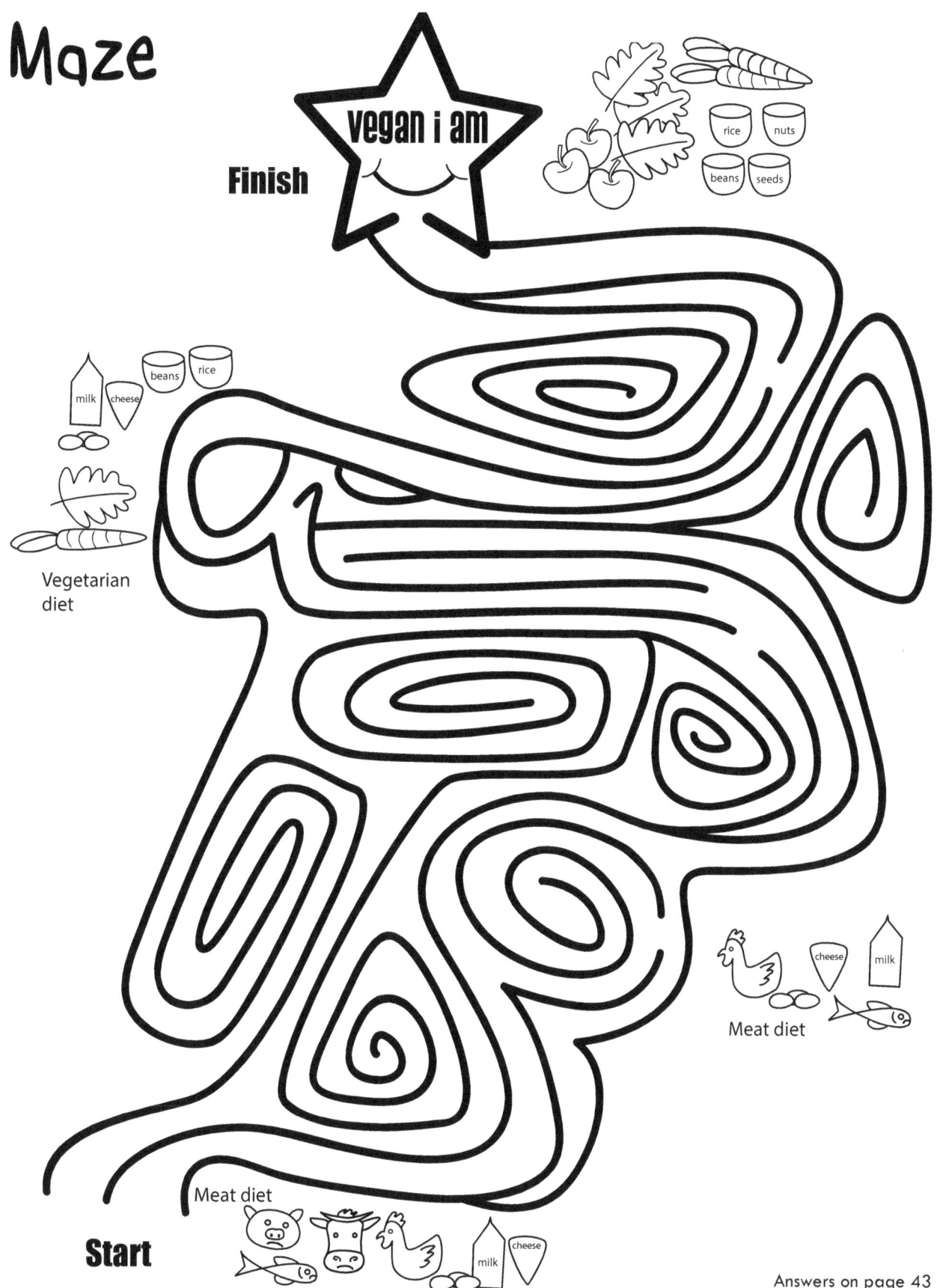

# Labyrinth

You cannot get lost and you cannot lose—just follow the path into the labyrinth with your finger and come back out.

When you travel though a labyrinth, you will feel how relaxing it can be!

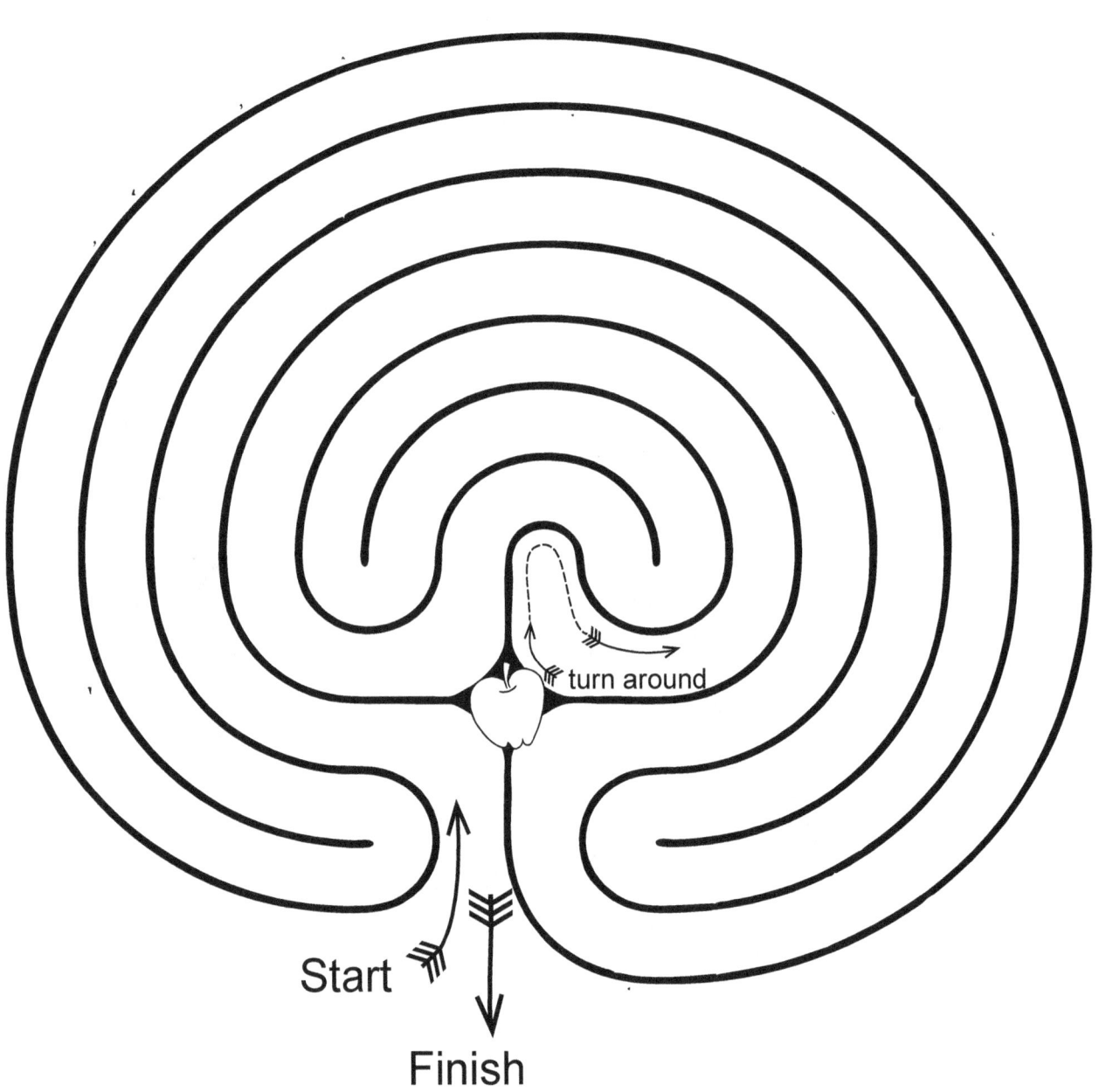

# Answers

Fruits and Vegetables Puzzle from page 39

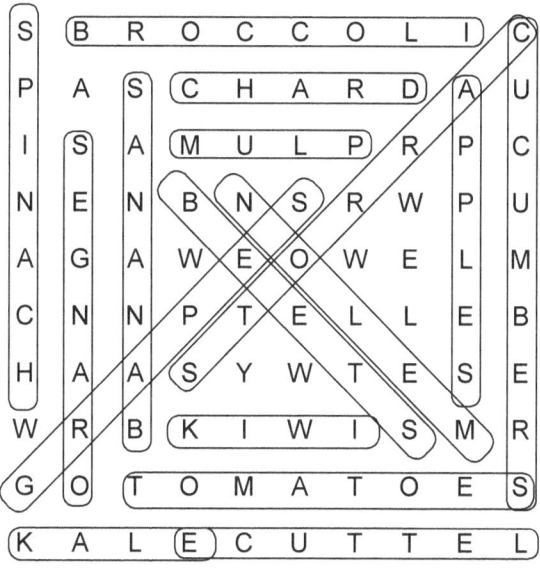

Famous Vegans Word Search from page 40

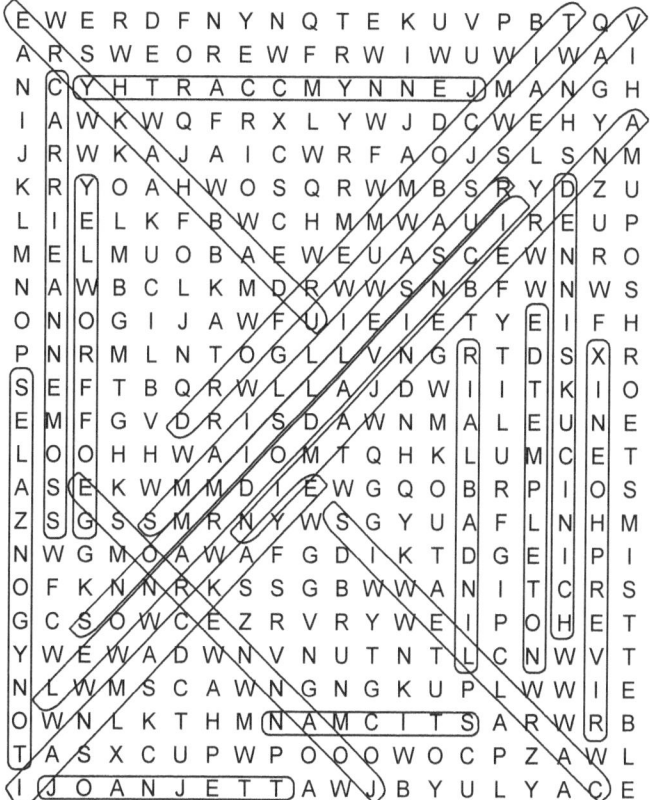

Maze from page 41

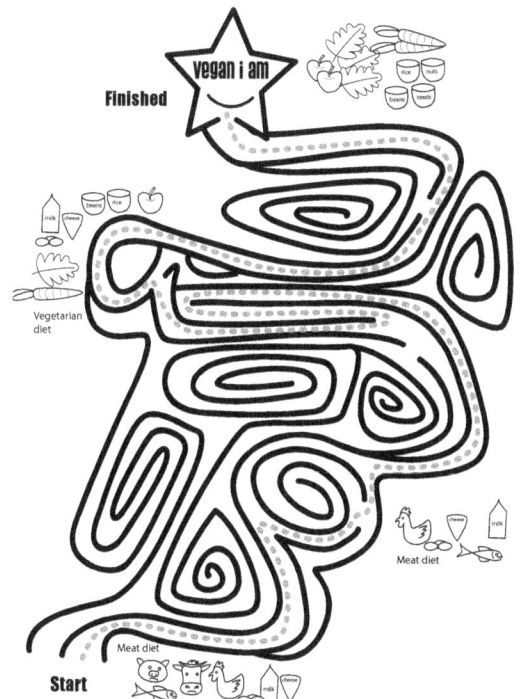

# Vegan food alternatives to animal products

## Dairy & Eggs

| animal products | vegan alternatives | vegan products |
|---|---|---|
| milk | soy, rice, almond, coconut, flax seed, hempseed milks | Silk, Edensoy, Organic Valley Earth Balance, Rice Dream, Good Karma<br>**WARNING:** These milk products cannot take the place of mother's milk or formulas for infants |
| eggs | egg replacement for baking, tofu for scrambled eggs, vegan egg | Ener-G, Bob's Red Mill Egg Replacer, Follow Your Heart VeganEggs |
| butter and margarine<br>Note: Many margarines contain whey, which is a milk product | olive oil, coconut oil, dairy-free margarines | Earth Balance, Smart Balance, Bryanna's Vegan Butter |
| sour cream | vegan sour cream | Tofutti Sour Cream, Follow Your Heart Vegan Gourmet Sour Cream |
| cheese | nutritional yeast, vegan cheese, cashew cheese | Go Veggie Grated Parmesan Style Topping, Daiya Vegan Cheese, Parma Nacheez (nacho cheese) |
| yogurt | soy | Silk, Whole Soy, Almond Dream |

## Meats

| animal products | vegan alternatives | vegan products |
|---|---|---|
| beef | seitan | Upton's Naturals, Vegetarian Plus Vegan Beef |
| ground beef | TVP (Textured Vegetable Protein), seitan | Fantastic Foods Joe Mix, Lightlife Smart Ground, Boca Crumbles, Beyond Meat |
| hamburger | seitan, grains, beans, tofu, TVP (Textured Vegetable Protein) | Yves Veggie Cuisine, Dr. Praeger's Sensible Foods, Quorn, Boca Burger, Organic Sunshine Barbeque Veggie Burgers, Gardenburger's Veggie Medley Veggie Burger, Wildwood, Hilary's |
| ham | seitan, tofu, tempeh<br>TVP (Textured Vegetable Protein) | Vegetarian Plus Vegan Ham Roll, Yves Veggie Cuisine Meatless Ham Deli Slices. |
| bacon | seitan, tofu, tempeh,<br>TVP (Textured Vegetable Protein) | Upton's Naturals, Wayfare Pig Out, Phoney Baloney Coconut Bacon, Stonewell Jerquee Cajun Bacon |
| chicken | seitan, tofu | Health is Wealth's Chicken-Free Patties, Gardein Buffalo Wings, Gardenburger Chik'n Grill |

## Meats

| animal products | vegan alternatives | vegan products |
|---|---|---|
| turkey | seitan, tofu | Tofurky, Vegetarian Plus Vegan Turkey |
| fish and seafoods | seaweed (**can be used to imitate taste of fish in many dishes**) | Sophie's Kitchen Breaded Fish Fillets, Vegetarian Plus Vegan Shrimp Roll, Vegetarian Plus Vegan Tuna |
| polish boys and sausages | seitan, tofu | Tofurky Gourmet Sausages, Gimme Lean Sausages |
| deli cold cuts | seitan, tofu | Light Life Smart Deli, Yves Veggie Cuisine, Tofurky |
| breakfast sausages | seitan, tofu, tempeh TVP (Textured Vegetable Protein) | Lightlife Smart Links Breakfast Sausage, Vegan Breakfast Sausage Patties by Sol Cuisine, Gardein Good Start Breakfast Patties, Stonewell Jerquee Cajun Bacon |

## Desserts, Bakery, Snacks

| animal products | vegan alternatives | vegan products |
|---|---|---|
| ice cream, ice cream bars and ice cream sandwiches | vegan ice creams made from coconut milk, soy milk, almond milk, rice milk and other milk substitutes. | So Delicious, Luna & Larry's Coconut Bliss, Tofutti, Rice Dream, Organic Rice Divine Chocolate Covered Vegan Ice Cream Bars |
| cookies | vegan cookies that use egg, butter and milk substitutes. | Liz Lovely, Bountiful Vegan, Michelle's Naturally, No Cookie, Uncle Eddie's Vegan Cookies |
| cakes | vegan cakes that use egg, butter and milk substitutes. | Cakelove, Dixie Diner's Club (cake mix) |
| candy and milk chocolate | vegan candies using milk free chocolates, cocoa, cacao, carob. | Good Greens Wellness Bar, Larabar, Raw Revolutions bars, Crispy Cat Candy Bars, The Lovely Candy Company, NuGo |
| pudding and gelatin | agar-agar flakes, carrageenan | Lieber's (vegan gelatin), Natural Desserts (vegan gelatin) Dr. Oetker (pudding), Eden (for your own recipe) |
| breads | vegan breads that use egg substitutes and no animal by-products | Rudi's Organic Bakery, Food for Life |

## Miscellaneous

| animal products | vegan alternatives | vegan products |
|---|---|---|
| honey, sugar and brown sugar | agave, yacon syrup, stevia, rice syrup, non bone-char sugar, maple syrup, date sugar, raw turbinado sugar, sucanat, coconut sweetener | Madhava Agave, Lundberg Sweet Dreams Organic Brown Rice Syrup, Navitas Naturals Organic Yacon Syrup, Wholesome Sweetners, Coombs Family Farm Organic Maple, Bob's Red Mill Date Sugar, Stevia In The Raw and Coconut Secret Raw Coconut Crystals |
| mayonnaise | vegan mayonnaise | Follow Your Heart Vegenaise, Earth Balance Mindful Mayo, Just Mayo by Hampton Creek, Nasoya's Vegan Nayonaise |

# More vegan food alternatives to try

| Other foods that may contain animal by-products | How to avoid these animal by-products |
|---|---|
| **Peanuts** shelled manufacturers use gelatin as a coating | Use peanuts in their shell |
| **Cake mixes** may contain animal fat | Choose cake mixes that do not contain beef fat or lard |
| **Hard candy** may be coated with "confectioner's glaze," derived from 'Shellac', a resin secreted from the lac bug | Read ingredients to avoid shellac and confectioner's glaze |
| **Bananas** may be sprayed with chitosan (from shellfish) | Buy organic bananas |
| **Bagels and bread** products may contain the enzyme L. Cysteine, a "dough conditioner" sourced from duck and chicken feathers. | Look for breads not containing dough conditioner |

The list above is a starter list of vegan foods that are available.

**PLEASE NOTE**
This list is just for alternatives to animal products. It is important to note that vegan foods on this list may or may not be healthy. Please check for sodium content, sugar, artificial colors, artificial flavors and GMOs. Note that 'natural flavors' may not be natural and may contain MSG, which is highly toxic. Vegan means free of animal products and does not mean healthy or healthier. A diet high in fruit and vegetables, nuts, seeds, legumes and grains in their original form (fresh, unprocessed) is highly recommended.

## REPLACE THIS        WITH THESE

## GO VEGAN!

# Ingredients to watch for

If you want to maintain a vegan diet, it is important to read the labels of the foods you eat. Learn what ingredients might be from animal sources so you can avoid them.

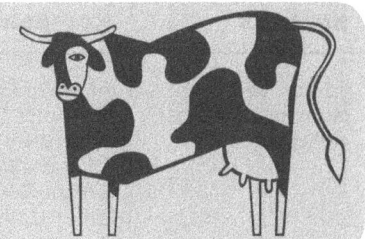

- 🐄    Ingredients that are of animal origin

- 🐄🍎    Ingredients that can be of animal or plant origins (look for the word "vegan" on the product label)

---

- 🐄🍎 **ALLANTOIN:** Contained in uric acid from cows and most mammals. Also in many plants (notably comfrey).

- 🐄🍎 **AMINO ACIDS:** Animal or plant sources (more information on page 51).

- 🐄🍎 **CALCIUM CARBONATE:** Found mainly in limestone, marble and chalk, bones, teeth, shells and plant ash.

- 🐄🍎 **CANE SUGAR:** Obtained by refining sugar cane using bone charcoal.

- 🐄 **CARMINE, NATURAL RED #4:** Red pigment from the crushed female cochineal insect. Reportedly 70,000 beetles may be killed to produce one pound of this red dye. Used in cosmetics and shampoos, as well as red apple sauce and other foods. May cause allergic reactions.

- 🐄 **CASEIN:** In "non-dairy" creamers and vegetarian cheeses (for instance, soy and almond), hair preparations, beauty masks and other cosmetics.

- 🐄 **GELATIN:** From cattle and hogs. Used as a thickener for fruit gelatins, puddings and jello, and in candies, marshmallows, cakes, ice cream and yogurts.

- 🐄 **LARD:** pig fat.

- 🐄🍎 **NATURAL FLAVORS:** Can be from animal or vegetable sources, but most often from an animal source.

- 🐄🍎 **RETINOL. VITAMIN A:** Can come from fish liver oil, egg yolks, or yellow and orange vegetables which contain carotene.

- 🐄 **WHEY:** from cow's milk.

---

Ingredient list from www.veganwolf.com

# Vegan Cosmetics, Hygiene and Fashion

| Cosmetics | |
|---|---|
| products | companies that sell vegan products |
| lipstick, eye liner, mascara and other makeup | Anastasia Beverly Hills, Kat Von D, Becca, Charlotte Tilbury, Josie Maran, Coverfx, OCC (Obsessive Compulsive Cosmetics), Thebalm, Bite, Face Atelier, It Cosmetics, Perfekt, Nudestix, Blinc, Cargo, Duwop, Eyeko, EcoTools |
| hair shampoo and conditioners | Gods Goodie's, Arbonne, OCC (Obsessive Compulsive Cosmetics) Pacifica, Nature's Gate, BWC (Beauty Without Cruelty), Billy Jealousy, ColorProof Evolved Color Care, Certain Dri |

| Hygiene | |
|---|---|
| deodorant | Bare Bones Body Care, Sparklehearts, Petit Vour, Herban Cowboy, Nature's Gate, EveryMan Jack Deodorant, Meow Meow Tweet |
| soaps and cleansers | The Fanciful Fox, SB (Simply Betsy) handmade soap (www.simplybetsycompany.com) Petit Vour, Herban Cowboy, Sam's Natural, Kirk's Natural, Adorn, Dr. Bronner's |
| toothpaste | Tom's of Maine, Davids, Jason, Dr. Bronner's, Nature's Gate, Hello, Himalaya, Desert Essence, Dr. Sharp |

| Clothing | |
|---|---|
| footwear | Inkkas, Zappos.com, Lulus, Avesu Vegan Shoes, Sole and Stone Vegan Footwear, Tieks by Gavrieli, Zulily, Ecouterre, Moo Shoes, Nicora Johns, Will's Vegan Shoes |
| clothes | Meaningful Paws, Ecotopiia, Delikate Rayne, Herbivore clothing, Della, Doctor Couture, Vaute Couture |
| coats | Vaute Couture, Asos, GGA (Girliegirlarmy), Charlotte Russe, Jill Milan |

# The 8 Essential Amino Acids

Protein is made from 22 amino acids. Our bodies can manufacture some of them, but there are 8 we can only get from the foods we eat; so they are known as essential amino acids. When we eat plant foods, the amino acids in the plants combine with those in our bodies to form protein.

We don't have to eat all 8 essential amino acids in one meal to meet our protein needs. We can eat them at different times of day, or even on different days. Amino acids are abundant in many plant foods. Eat a variety of plant foods, and you will have plenty of protein from which to build strong muscles, tendons, and ligaments. Protein deficiencies are rare.

| Foods with essential amino acids | | | |
|---|---|---|---|
| Tryptophan | chocolate, oats, bananas, dates, peanuts | Leucine | sesame seeds, peanuts, dry lentils |
| Lysine | green beans, lentils, soybeans, spinach, amaranth | Isoleucine | lentils, seeds, soy, wheat, almonds |
| Methionine | whole grains | Threonine | beans, nuts, seeds |
| Valine | grains, mushrooms, peanuts, soy protein | Phenylalanine | almonds, avocados, lima beans, peanuts, seeds |

# FOOD AND VEGAN DOCUMENTARIES

- The Ghosts in Our Machine
- 101 Reasons to Go Vegan
- The Superior Human
- Forks Over Knives
- Peaceful Kingdom
- Live and let Live
- PlantPure Nation
- Meet Your Meat
- Meat the Truth
- Cowspiracy
- Simply Raw
- Vegucated
- Earthlings
- Speciesism
- Food Inc.
- Blackfish
- Eating
- Unity

# Internet Resources for Vegan Information

Facebook group
"Vegan All the Way"
www.happycow.net
www.vegsource.com
www.vegan.com
www.vegweb.com
www.veganyumyum.com
www.veganbodybuilding.com
www.veganoutreach.org
www.thevegetariansite.com
www.greenfriends.com

www.ethicalplanet.com
www.souleyvegan.com
www.vegansociety.com
www.peta.org
www.chooseveg.com
www.veganpeace.com
www.myveganplanet.com
www.veganclub.com
www.trulyvegan.net
www.livevegan.org
www.veganwolf.com

www.veganhealth.org
www.veganangela.com
www.circlefmoms.com
www.onegreenplanet.com
www.foodforthesoul.opare.net
www.bostonveg.org
www.joyfulvegan.com
www.vegansouls.com
www.caft.org.uk

# Glossary

**Amino Acids**
Building blocks of proteins. 22 amino acids come together to form protein. Humans need to obtain 8 of these amino acids from their diets.

**Carnivore**
A flesh-eating animal (for example, a lion or a shark)

**Deficiency**
The lack of a vital nutrient, such as a specific vitamin or mineral.

**Global Warming**
A rise in the earth's temperature based on the "greenhouse effect." It happens when greenhouse gases (carbon dioxide, water vapor, nitrous oxide and methane) trap heat and light from the sun in the earth's atmosphere. The rise in temperature hurts many people, animals and plants. Over time, many species of animals cannot take the change, so they die out.

**Plant-Based Diet**
A diet that focuses on eating foods that come from plants, such as whole grains, nuts, seeds, legumes, fruits and vegetables. For the healthiest plant-based diet, some people choose to eliminate or limit processed plant foods like white flour, sugar and oils.
*A person on a plant based diet may or may not support animal entertainment (such as zoos and circuses), animal testing and the wearing of animal skins or fur.*

**Vegan**
A person who does not consume any animal flesh or animal by-products like eggs, milk, yogurt, cheese, sour cream, butter or honey. Vegans respect animals by not wearing furs, wool, or even leather, and by not supporting animal testing. Also, vegans will not support businesses that use animals as a form of entertainment like zoos, circuses, horse races, etc. Vegans advocate against factory farming, humane meat and any other practice that involves exploitation and cruelty toward animals.

**Vegetarian**
A person who does not consume any animal flesh in their diet. This rules out not only pork and beef, but also chicken, turkey and fish. Some vegetarians do eat dairy, eggs or honey, as explained in the definitions below.

| | |
|---|---|
| **Lacto Vegetarian** | A person who does not eat animal flesh, and who may include dairy products like milk, cheese or butter in their diet—but no eggs. |
| **Ovo Vegetarian** | A person who eats no animal flesh and no dairy, but may include eggs. |
| **Lacto-ovo Vegetarian** | A person who eats no animal flesh, but consumes eggs and dairy. |

# Vegan Notes

# Vegan Notes

www.ingramcontent.com/pod-product-compliance
Lightning Source LLC
Chambersburg PA
CBHW081022040426
42444CB00014B/3319